D.O.N.U.T.S

Miles Randall

authorHOUSE®

AuthorHouse™
1663 Liberty Drive
Bloomington, IN 47403
www.authorhouse.com
Phone: 1-800-839-8640

Published by AuthorHouse 2/20/2013

ISBN: 978-1-4817-1382-5 (sc)
ISBN: 978-1-4817-1383-2(e)

Library of Congress Control Number: 2013902671

This book is dedicated in loving memory of Stephanie Renee Randall

Preface (Gift of Light)

Steam from radiators
Beams of clarity
Radiance
Her beauty is perfect
With gestures of music
All these features
An undefined uniqueness
Want to search the genealogy
to find the psychology of her mind
A confined rage blinds the stage
The symbolism of fire ignites the starter
Part of me suspends upon her alternator
Generations of electricity from her eccentricity
The ability to bend time and write lines
comes from the heart
Knowing I will love her for a lifetime
As forever the sun still shines
This light of mine will see steps
Left or right
As every direction points to the one
who takes my breath away
The Milky Way
Silk haired woman
The subscription to despair is no longer there
With each ounce of air I breathe
Elevates the bounce of love

For this dove that
I call the one
The ruby to my soul
Such enchantment that all will know the arrangement
Engaged
A page after the chapters of her heart
Knowing I loved her from the start

Table of Contents

A Song

This song is for you
Yet to be titled
What is your name
Is love the answer to this pain
Happiness on the day you came
Joy counters the rain
Eyes blossom to the scent of your aroma
Former shackles can no longer tame feelings
When cupid raises a building
Love develops a higher ceiling
Dust settles upon the mountain tops
The search for her never stops
As the shadows draw close
So does her smell
A taste like no other
An odor like desire
A flame of passionate fire
keeps the will determined
The soul burns for her fumes
As the tune starts to play
This song is for you
Yet to be titled
What is your name
In her heart lies my vitals
Searching for a rhythm hoping she finds home
For in her womb

I am reborn
Formed to love her
Care and nurture
In dreams
I am the painter
And she is the brush that touches my life

Abstract

These words are abstract paintings
Searching for meaning
Feed me more of your graffiti
Draw the path to freedom
For captivity is devouring the soul
Who has the power
Tell me
Who is the controller of these hours
Masters at work
Starter of shift
Where is the wheel to turn life around
When life is down
Who bears the crown
Thy sitter of the mount
Lead me to your kingdom
Show me them keys
Open up cays
Elevate those bays
Levitate with your eyes
See past disguises
Rise to the domain of the mind truest form
Clear the confinement
Unlock some wisdom
Pocket the lint
Eliminate all dust
For clarity is a must

Knowing these words are abstract paintings
Finding a meaning
Leading a cause
As destiny is much more than a store
Blood of a heart impure
Dwelling on surface water
Life will endure
Unveiling the source
Abstract
Nothing is for sure

An Ocean

Can you be the ocean
The one who elevates
Many from the bottom to the top
Your drive is non-stop
With beauty so incredible
From a few drops you were conceived
Who would have ever believed
The ocean could be our savior
Every day one seeks you out in favor
Beyond your exterior
Lies deeper thoughts
Hidden visions
An ocean filled with revelations
Holds the key to our salvation
Once again I ask
Can you be the ocean
The center of attention
The journey of mankind
Lies deep beneath your waters
As we continue to cross those borders
Change will come at the very moment of your order
An emotion like no other
The ocean I dreamt of in my dreams
Has come to life
As its beauty gleams from a distance
The oceans persistence is forever
Embedded in the soul

Anew

She thirsts in my dying rain
The first to ask thy name
A rebirth to once again
Ignite the flame that was left in ashes
Traces in a path
Remind me of the flashes
The former glory
Can I change life like a game
Normal settings
Portal ready
Entering my minstrel show
No I am not a laughing stock
For I am the rock that bears her name
I hold her
when she sleeps like a bed frame
And tell her
You are the mother of my child
My better counterpart
The start of my belief to fly once again
Part of the wave that liquidizes my oxygen
Through every breath of these walking steps
I could feel your heart beating
Searching for answers
Stop
For I hear the presence of your coming
You are never alone

As together to be
We are destined
The worst is over
Let happiness begin once again

Beautiful Temptation

Beauty is temptation
Her look sends shockwaves down my spine
Information her name I seek
A feeling like the inside of a microwave heating up
Repeated thoughts
The smell that comes from her cloth
With lips so soft
Turns me on when I am off
Intimate desires burn within my soul
A hold on me so strong
Her eyes read my mind
Brainstorm
As she transforms my movements
Control
Her voice is like music
Composed
With lips the color of rose
I suppose she knows as I stare
Love paints my air
Compare
To her no one near
I fear the end is here
As her love is no longer there
Beauty is her name
Every drop in my body
Lusts for her rain

For this rain is the solution to this pain
On my mind she's in my brain
Uncontrollable is this hold
That she has on my soul
Every move I make she knows
How am I supposed to surprise
When this beauty of sunshine
Sees right through these eyes
Tell me why
Beauty is such a temptation
I hesitate
As you walk by
Trying to gather my speech
So close
Yet far out of reach
Each step you take I yearn
About this beauty I am learning
For determined I am
To one day hold your hand
And whisper melodies of sweet caress in your ear
Your air becomes my love
My love for you is an addiction
Turned into affection
Shocked by your rejection
Beauty is temptation
Still tempted
As her thoughts arouses suspicion
With attraction like a magnet
Her love is like the sweetest drug
Addiction
Makes one simply crave for her thirst
The first thought that enters my mind

Is this beauty
A beauty as sweet as pumpkin pie
With eyes that never lie
Temptation floating in the sky
Everywhere she goes
She leaves a scent as fresh as the rose
That grew from concrete
The missing piece to the puzzle
This beauty known as temptation
Makes my life so complete

Believer

Moments
Entrapment in loneliness
Steadfast holiness
A believer in sight
Parallels between skies and heights
Distances unseen past the sun's light
Flight from mind
Wings of no kind
Style
As sensual as fine wine
Facilitator of range
Catalytic membranes
The heart of a believer
Eternal flame
Lost like baggage claim
Rain has no drain
Stoppage deemed insane
Moving past things mundane
A sound believer in the unbelievable
Strange
Thoughts contained
Togetherness like clouds
Attained
Pieces rearranged
Puzzles with no solve
Evolved

A world resolve
Calmness
As the storm surrounds
Victory looms around
A believer once lost
Now is found

Broken Wings
(A letter from my heart)

I will always have you in my heart
Knowing I must depart
I will continue to love you from start to finish
Not even a shattered mirror could damage us
The world changes
But we will forever remain the same
I write this hoping to see you again
Happiness is what I want for you
And not the pain
If I could regain my composure
Maybe I will change for the better
If love was just a letter
I would have had it all put together
Not one to say never
For you will always be a part of me
Like a birds feather
Time is the essence of my soul
As the memories of us
I will forever hold on to
Part of you will always be with me
For you helped mold me
Into the person I am today
Thank you for sharing your world
Who ever knew that caring about someone
could feel this good
Knowing what I should have done
Up until the person I have now become

What was once two
Now is one
Hopefully one day
We will once again rise like the sun
Life for us has only just begun
Here we stand amidst the pressures
Using the greatest treasure
Each other hearts
Into making it through the hardest parts of love
In order to rise above
The downfalls that we may encounter
Lets us remember
To use these showers of love
As gifts to lift us
From this strain of pain
So that we can forever remain the same
No matter the distance
In order to fight off life's changing lanes
Up we came from this beautiful history
Called our past
In the back of our minds
Saying this love we can make it last
Forever in a day
May your heart always be with me
And never led astray
I will pray for us
Mentally
Physically
And
Spiritually
Why to some our love remains a mystery
Only we know the chemistry
Not just an experiment
But an unforgettable experience
I like to call joy

Broken Wings 2
(A letter from my heart)

The love that we once experienced is no more
For our time has expired
But the one thing I still feel is inspired
Because the love took us places
Never to be thought of
Day by day I ponder
Over the sweet memories of you
I will forever keep these everlasting thoughts
No matter the cost
For even though we got lost
In the mazes of love
The feeling of each other's touch
Took us above and beyond
Time and space
A journey of epic proportions
Blinded by distortion
Love was never meant to be an obstacle
But a moving force unstoppable
Proving that anything is possible
Beyond a shadow of a doubt
As we made our leap of faith
Into the shadows of the unknown
And placed our lives in the hands
Of a four letter word
Not knowing the outcome
Or if we would emerge victorious

But until that time comes
We will forever remain glorious
Over the gifts that love has showered us with
Never should one feel guilt
Towards the heartbreak that love brings
For the foundation we have built
Will forever be like the patchwork in a quilt
With the memories forever remaining in our hearts
Until once again
the spirit of love will reunite us
Like the strongest fire of passion and desire
As high as the heavens
With love holding us up in the air
like a hot air balloon
Waiting as that special day comes
When we will walk the aisle as bride and groom
Destined we have become to be
To have heavens light shower down upon us
The feelings of love and trust
Have brought us closer than ever before
It was made clear the night at the altar
That together we would be forever
Our vows stated
Never will shall we fall apart
But use each other's hearts
From start to finish
So that our souls will not diminish
Memories will never vanish
Every moment will be cherished
Until the end our days
We will continue to grow
As we pray for happiness
From here on out
Amen

Care Package

Love you
I do
For it is my call of duty
The moment you came into my life
It was more than a special delivery
But a celebration through eternity
Like that special key one never gets to turn
As the fire that never really burns
So determined to have you
Even in death
My ashes will still love in this urn
So many pages to turn
But as I turn to you
Never do I want to turn away
Just come closer
As I will love you infinity times over
Your knight and shining armor
Is here to save the day
For I am your care package
I am the light in your darkness

The hand that holds you through your walks in the park
You are never alone
For you are always in my heart
And forever on my mind
One who is sweet and kind
No hill or incline
Will stop me from prestige
A protection never out reach
An affection that in always in your keep
No other way to be
I am your care package
Even when your sleep
So may you be at peace
Goodnight

Castle Walls

No pretending
Surrender
Love you
I do
Pain consumes thoughts
Sleepless nights in tombs
As grey skies loom
Dreams of better realities
Silenced by the gloom
Sadness covers a room like travel does
Smells of former fragrances lingers over these fingertips
As crushed chips do
Dipped sauces
Covers the entrance like the fortress rule
Rules the mind
A solitary confined cry
The never answered why
With pain deeper than hurt
Feelings not only resonate through skirts
Beneath castle walls ceilings convey hidden truths
Beyond verdicts of truth
Justice has not served me well
Flotation device
Destination
Hell

Cherry Red

Kiss the lips of the cherry red
Exchange spit
As the candles of love lifts spirits
Handle the passion of love making with finesse
Unwind into that perfect dress
Drinker of finer wines
Put your taste to use
Cut a cloth of your beauty
Paste the world with a lovely image
For no one can match your splendor
More beautiful than the season of summer
Celestial paint reigns supreme
Portrait of beauty
Object of desire
Cherry red lips
The color of fire
Can I taste the odor
Width of passion
Just want a piece of your love
Slices of romantic action
At every intersection
Cherry red lips
The heart of my affection

Daydream

They say dreaming is believing
Take me back to a time
A time when life had meaning
And my mother's heart was still beating
My soul's bleeding
The heart defeated
Many days I feel weak
Eyes closed
But no sleep
Feelings of a lost sheep
Looking for shepherds
No comfort like the loving from a mother
If mirrors could feel my pain
Then they would cry too
Never again will I be whole
Hopefully God will see me through
Every step taken
I daydream
As if you were still here

A dream comes true
At every seam
Your love for sewing was abundant
As the patches of your love
Left a permanent stitch in the hearts of many
A thousand candles in memory of your love
Rekindling a perfect spirit
Your heart was pure
So much pain you endured
If only cancer had a cure
Looking for answers
Days without you
Are cold winters
Every room I enter
Memories of you resurface
Black curtains hung from your windows
Candles were your crowning jewel
Like an emerald
Just to see you one more day
I would never let go
As I close my eyes and daydream
We danced the night away once more

Daydream 2

Still dreaming
Hope to see you soon
My heart is screaming out in pain
As these tears cover more spaces than rain
From the window pane
I see sketches of your name
Forever embedded
We are one in the same
Every lane crossed
Memories cross my mind
Hard to find the words to say
Time is an explosive mine
Paper is the never-ending line
If we were paper
We would never run out of time
Through my life
I have seen shine
But more darkness
More falls than rises
Still my soul rises
Hoping for sunrise

Smell of fresh air
Even as the circumstances is made unclear
I daydream
Hoping for a way out of despair
Wishing my mother was still here
Waking up everyday
Wondering if I still care
Pondering thoughts like a sick cough
Reminiscing about loved ones lost
Listening for the final moments
As the lights go off
I daydream
For a better tomorrow
An end to all sorrows
If only happiness will let borrow
There would not be so much horror
Every mirror is a reminder
of each step rendered
One more road to cross
Another journey to follow
I daydream
Wishing my dreams were not far away

Definition

Words from the heart
Nobody can define your art
Pictures painted
Glow in the dark symbols
Release of flow when the light dimmers
Peak the heights
The moment of your room enters
Sight of new ventures
Temperatures rising
Rising like the sun
Beginning of light
Ending a life
Start of anew
Staying true
Living proof
Riser of tops
Layer of roofs
Always more to do
Hearts focused like a locomotive
Streamline the mind
For one day you will find
Destiny alongside of a train track
Look deeper
Stretch the lines
Sketch an art
The perfect picture

Tales of a surface dweller
A teller with beautiful stories
Art opens up invisible doors
The start of something pure
Water will endure
Heat shall remain
The vast will attain
Victory is once again

Dementia

Give me a moment to shine freely
When you say you love me
Tell me you are not kidding
Sell me a dream
Paint the picture so serene
That the grassy green covers the eyelids
Hover the lies with shields
So that I may be at your beckon will
Second my thoughts
Kill the first right
Night my day
Brainstorm the path
Throw seeds in the way
Let me grow in the cameras of your flash
An aura of the past
is no more of memory
Touched by your energies
I am paralyzed
By the rise of beautiful eyes
When they enters mines
No danger in mind
Even if your demeanor is of proximity mines
Time waits for no one
Yet I wait for you
As a slave waits for their master
Just want to pick from your cotton

And taste the water from your fountain
Even though the youth part is a dream
I love you by all means
Though we are far apart
Dementia
You still have my heart

Destiny's Believer

Butterfly kisses
Flight from sky
Reborn existence
Persistence without resistance
Fear no longer existent
Gifts for the world
A Santa's presence
Drops from chimney's
The comfort of home residences
Fireplace burning
Yearning eyes ponder over great wonders
Seven seas
Start of a dream
Beginnings of a believer
Soul searching
Newfound research
Always striving
Words come alive like ventriloquists
For the moment I speak
The will
Will start the wheel
Slowly turning
Pieces of a yarn
Piece the masterpiece
Ease of tensions arouse suspicion
Listen

As the words spread like margarine
Caution
Belief will find you
Often
Relief from pain
Struggle is healing
Belief has no ceiling
Relief has cause
For destiny lies within us all

E.O.D (Evolving Over Dreams)

My mind is stuck on you
Bubblegum kisses
No need for three wishes
For you are everything desired
Upon the pillars of your love
Built is an empire
Journeying across seas
Surviving swarms of bee's stings
Nothing will keep away the thirst for your love
Upon thou hand
As I lay these vowels
In hopes of never throwing in the towel
Climbing over mounds
Moving mountains
Distance has no existence
As my mind is stuck on you
Lost in thoughts
Cloudy skies

Dream filled nights spent hearing the voice of your whispers
In hopes of glittery eyes and diamond sparkles
Replacing dark holes with new patches
The spark of new joules
An entry of new light
Skies unlimited
Cries of euphoria
Exploration through higher dreams
Push has no seam
Believer of meaning
The fevers relieving
An elevator of life
Enter my elevator
Ruler of these thoughts
An up and down sensation
The extravaganza of life's roller coaster
Revisited memories
Energy of youth
Actors of childhood
Shades in form factoring growth
Steady evolving over dreams
The bestowal of all hope

Elements

I want to write poetry see
Emotions as
As the thoughts thought in sleep
Dreams of peace
Destiny's reach
A reality so complete
No other fantasy can compete
Oh how sweet the sound
Of harmonies harmonic compounds
Surrounding clouds
Blue skies
Magic carpet rides
Distilled pictures
The moment of sunrise
Enter my canyon
See sights the eyes will pleasure
Beyond measures lie treasures
Once a formality
Forever realizing realities
No longer casualties
But birds with wings
Soaring the skies
Infinite limits in flight
Sceneries painted with beautiful nights
Beginning of life
Start of anew
Foundations set as fireproof
Water
The everlasting truth

Exile

Free my mind
Oh healer of the blind
Give me a piece of your shine
So that I may illuminate mankind
And lift them from these hard times
Eyes of truth
A voice with flutes
I salute you my gracious one
As I begin the transformation to your elevation
Concentrate
For the path of the unknown is never straight
Time is of the essence
Granting passage through this maze known as life
A sudden high
Blue skies
Crystal balls telling lies to all
Fortunes in the form of fireballs
Scorching
Death is approaching
Steady hoping losing faith
Save me
From this cycle of hate
Break the mold
Release me from this cold
Change the code
Make a way to open what was once closed

Used to be known
Now a former shell
Clone
In a world all alone
Hope is forever gone

Felony Love

Love is a felony
The undying soul is in jeopardy
In tune with her harmonies
Sweet voices no longer sing to me
The fruits of her love have no share
From the rear I watch
As another man holds what I love so dearly
Clearly attraction is a mystery
History lesson
Don't judge a book by its cover
Can't help myself
For I love her pages
Every chapter moves a crowd like stages
Love
Her love
A ringworm
Contagious

The outrageous pulsating heartbeat
Lust the unprotected sex
Having this jewel is a must
Crowing moments left in dust
For when love really mattered
Ladders broke
Stuck in the puddles of my own sorrows
Dreams have become the worthless tomorrows
Love is a felony
Music no longer sings to me
The tune of her melody
Brings sadness to my memories
Escape is the only remedy
To relieve me from this felony called
Love

Flowers

Solely focused on the power
One has never seen the will of these flowers
A seed stimulates the growth
Never could we emulate
But only hope to participate
Faith has led us this far
If only we could touch a star
Then you would see how a flower smiles
All the while
The humans are in exile
Waiting to be freed from captivity
Watch as these flowers resume their daily activities
Growing past prosperity
Here lies the moment of clarity
A flower takes on many melodies
Pain has a remedy
The flower shines through eternity

Future Legend

As the words get deeper
Sleep no longer has residence
Existence only exists
On the basics of persistence
Resistance to struggle
Has no merit
Time keeps passing
Ways are become shorter
Distance has no miles
A boundary serves no bondage
Paying homage to the greats of the past
A future legend arises from the grass
Out to the landscape
In search for greener pastures
A master of art departs
From what was once was
To be place above
Clouds and great skies
Highs of incredible peaks
Reach has pushed the envelope
Evolution develops a brain
Rain has settled in the terrain
Drops seeping through windowpanes
Water fills the soul
Jars hold
Words capture
After has no end

Heavenly Woman

Are you beautiful
As the light touches the sky
Heaven becomes the color of your eyes
A new world awakens
Shaped by the elegance of your skin
Brought up by radiance
Your light shines brighter than the sun
Never knew this day would come
The makings of a perfect creature known as woman
Could place smiles on faces
Oh woman of glory
The chapter of a beautiful story
A beginning with truth
An after with no end
A mixture of sweet blends
Topped in your fashionable ways
Wrapped in attire of best dressed
The way you move peaks my interest
Just want to hold you in sweeping distance
A love for you so deep
Having no resistance
A gift of deliverance
Heavenly woman the up-lifter of my spirits
Set us free from calamity
Show us the way not known to many
Continue great harvester of precious seeds

Producer of fine fruits
To all women
You are the flute
The composer of sweet melodies
Fine tuner of harmony
Forever yours eternally
Undying Love

Heavenly Woman 2

Woman of mystery
The hope inside of my dreams
Flights cannot capture your heights
A true beauty with heavenly posture
The moisture of your tender skin
Can penetrate the heart
of the coldest of men
Your love is like the ocean
The coolest breeze
Just want to be in the sight of your eyes
Heavenly woman
Creator of what is elegant
Intelligence speaks highly of you
Valleys peak in your midst
Mountains grow taller whenever you smile
Springs develop into fountains upon your arrival
Vitals sync together with rhythm to perform dance
Your love is music
The perfect note
Composer of harmonic waveforms
Heavenly Woman
The mother of birth
Your value is of the highest worth
Every moment is spent thinking of you
Sinks do not express the deepness of your love
Impressed by your smell

Heavenly Woman
You are the flower
A tale of growth

Heavenly Woman 3

Woman of heaven
Caretaker in flight
Internal butterfly
With beautiful melodies like a lullaby
Birth of a lovely rise
A plateau higher than dove's sky
Sweeter than the smell of oven baked pie
Woman of power
Still I rise
Maya Angelou voice
Choice words
Beginnings of unique
Heavenly woman
All that is sweet
Roses in a flower
Love at the altar
Open up coves
As your essence spreads like the water
From the canals heaven shines its light
Enriched in destiny
Out from the chemistry
Woman of heaven
A sophisticated science
Caretaker in appliance
Stoves of warmth
Provider with charm

The one with loving arms
Infinite beauty
Sight for soaring eyes
Scenery of a beautiful night
That special star in the sky
Greater than any constellation prize
The beauty of heaven's creation
As your population rises
So does your love
An everyday surprise
Oh heavenly woman
The Christmas in my life
Your gifts are truly wonderful
And so is your soul
Everyday pieces of gold
The uplifter of souls
Your beauty is passion
As is your mind
Numbers for the heaven in your ways
One is for the birth of a child
Two for the brightness of your smile
Three for your essence in style
From out the Nile
Your Egyptian eyes rise like the pyramids
Heavenly woman
You are forever my destiny

Human Nature

Bird's fly
Love spreads its wings through the night
Precipitation
Natural highs
Eccentric waveforms floating in the sky
Beautiful melodies like lullabies
The sight of loving eyes
A baby bring born
Tears of happiness from a beautiful morning
Sigh
Relief
In the belief
Believers still exist
Mother nature embraces us with a kiss
An elegant plot with the perfect twist
Growth of a generation fertilizes a surface
Life has greater purpose
Deep inside each person
Lies artifacts of ancestral trace
A drawing of epic wonder flourishes the land
A world so vast
The makings from a higher mask
Creates the moldings bearing the mass
A hole representing see through
Human nature
In the form of sweet dew
Civilization made brand new

Human Nature 2

The epilogue
Love is forever with us all
From humble beginnings
To the honey
Emotions like the bee sting
Tales of beautiful beginnings
A never-ending story
Dreams of big white dogs
Penetrating clouds
Cinematic rainfalls
Eclipsing the tundra
Growth of flowers
Epic wonder
Pondering thoughts
A human mind flourishes a flower
Visions like mountains grow taller
Everyday sites becomes new heights
In light human nature
The God giving illuminator
Forever embedded
Faces consonant with prominence
Vows to the skies
I am human
And
Nature is the harmonica
A song of life

Human Nature 3 (The Life Poem)

A beautiful capture
Landscapes over raised structures
The beginning of life
God's paint touches
Human nature clusters
One of many wonders
Oceans conjures up such exquisiteness for the pondering eye
Look to the skies
Clouds stand amidst the heavenly heights
Along songs speak to us
Providing rhythms for the path
Colliding colors formulates the perfect chemistry
The sweet odor of human nature
Embraces walls like living quarters
Water
The essence of life
Purified souls derive knowledge from speech
Human nature the definition beyond reach
Life
The key to openings not found in doors
Hope is locked away
Secured
Destiny by design
Life is yours
Finding self
Blending soul

Perfect mixture
Surface dweller
Your light sparks the fixture

Illuminating Shadow

Why the world hates my shine
Many roads crossed
Darkness blinds
As grass pretends to be green
But behind the scenes
lies a different means of transformation
Confirmation
Transportation on the way
In the meantime I pray
For safer destinations
Elevation beyond elevators
Repairs not suitable for commentators
Hands on struggle
In the midst of these puddles lie deeper hurdles
Searching for certain
Windows closed
All I see is curtains
Fingerprints of depressed souls
Flesh reopening's
Heart failure no longer in control
Who has the key to unlock illumination
So shadows can follow
The walls they speak to me
False idols they try to preach to me
But I walk alone
For I am my own
Illuminating shadow

Labyrinth

Challenges through mazes
Life phases corrects vision
Contact lenses
Focused on climbs up fences
Mind density fills water
The matter still gathers material
Imperial thoughts
Heart of king
Thrones to future heirs
The air becomes music
Beginning of sing
Fusion syncs together
Mind
Body
And
Soul
Thus the whole being is completed
No forms necessary

Confirmed for a rebirth
Finding forever
Possible think search
Darkness lurks
Flesh of the bleeding hurts
Struggle is the worse
Confided in a heart that no longer works
Shaded area grays
Favorite images faded away
The memories of today
Dates further back to the yesterday
Through the labyrinth
Schemes against the soul
Elaborate
Themes of a lost scene
Catching glimpses of former self
Like an old dream

Love Punch

Dipped in red
Her cherry lips blossomed
like gospels at the Sunday morning church
From the mountains perch
Stands a heart
In search for love
Not just any love
But the love from her love punch
A future with a touch
Destiny floating atop of the aspen
I write for the passion of a woman's skin
The smoothness of a pen begins with a few love notes
The meaning of eyes has hope
As this woman
The leader of a dream
Penetrates my heart with a scope
Special is this rose
I suppose
I will purpose
In hopes she will comes closer
to the composer of these thoughts of her
Frozen is body in wait of heat
Life becoming complete is an afterthought
Without the love from her love punch
As a bowl of cereal without a captain
The mind sinks into the milk

Without the experience of taste
All other love is a waste
But the love from her love punch
Brings me back to that special place

Love Secret

I got a love secret
It involves you and me
Along with the moon and the stars
The way your mood ring changes color
An aura like no other
Blissful wonder
Through the chambers of my soul
Your name bears the same name as my aunt
Where are you Sheila
Tell me
Where are you
There you are
Floating in my dreams
Gloating at my screams
A feeling so serene
Not even I can tell you what it means
The proposed teller of these things
A seller of secrets
Yet love bears no price
Throwers of the rice
But there is no wedding tonight
Has love lost me like my jheri curl
A bald ego
Just need a perfect woman
To match my imperfect world
Patches in mind remind me of the deepest secrets

Love does not weaken
Instead its strengthens
Arms stretched out waiting
Until my true love awakens

Love's Wing

Formed from beauty's wing
Heaven only knows her name
Pitted against the flames of love
Doves commence
The ceremonious harmony brought by epic wonder
Raises the eyebrows of those in attendance with splendor
The burning desire of love
Through the coldest of winters
As forever our entrance will have the same paths
A journey crafted through struggle
of beautiful beginnings
Real love has no ending
Vowels without consonants
Loving you times seven like continents
In every place constantly
The reminder of my heart
From start to finish
Souls invested
In hopes of gaining
Immortality
Moving past the fallacies and the tragedies
Open is a galaxy
Love is the allergy
Flight from mind's strategy
In the midst of perfect company
Love's wing is the district leading to luminous bliss

The passion of a midnight kiss
Can make a star shine
Oh so bright

Moonlight Kiss

A butterfly sensation
Sparked from the temptation of one's lips
Can make even the sexiest hips tingle
That one single kiss can change destiny
At a moment's notice
And make many swarm to it like locusts
A sting in the form of a perfect kiss
Leaves a permanent bliss
That of which you cannot resist
Open your eyes and realize
That you have been connected to passion
An action that speaks louder than words
Can be heard from across the room
As a silent whisper
Giving you the most pleasurable jitters
Bringing a warm glitter smile to your face
This in fact is the end of your chase
We have no time to waste
As this kiss takes us into space
Love face to face
My place becomes your place
Romantic sounds playing in the background
Smooth vibrant voices
Creating temptation for your minds deepest aspirations
In preparation of the most epic
Climatic stimulation
Stimulating from a moonlight kiss

Mother's Son

Looking at what I have done
Things I am not too proud of
A sinner with no will power
Yet as a mother your love is like a flower
Too much stress I cannot cope
In your final hours
I am losing hope
Whenever I needed you gave
Even though I misbehave
You forgave me
Things I took for granted
Only added to the damage
Not like I was suffering from famine
Everything you could
You supplied
Mom you truly are a beautiful history
What you said holds true
When I'm gone you're going to miss me
There are many nights I cry
On the day you died
A part of me died with you
I truly do miss you
Forever until eternity
But what remains is your spirit
A spirit that grows inside of me
If you could see me now
Then you will see what I am destined to be
To make you proud
With my fist in the air
I will shout out the letters of your name

My Own World

The world has no entry
Pantries no longer hold bread
Images carry the same mold
My own world still the only choice
The power of voice
Freedom with struggle
Beginnings in puddles
Pain rains its sadness
In pursuit of happiness
Climbs to the top
Materials gathered
Father of wisdom
Root has emerged
Perched on the idea of verge
No force can penetrate course
My mind's syllabus
Take note
The intro of higher plateau
Mind stimulated through plants
Each seed feeds the growth
Never needed to vote
For my heart is president
And the soul keeps residence
A glowing smile is evident
Slowing down time bears no crown
Carefree

No clocks in town
Beautiful flock
My own shepherd's
Picker of spots
A special place dipped in leopard
My own world
The new forever

No Superstar

The cries of yesterday
Not too far from distant mind
Shattered ambitions
The start of a misguided revolution
Confided in confidants
Not suited for resolution
The mistaken many
A forsaken few
Intensity fuels the fire
Divided desires
Infiltrates an empire
City of ruins
The once conceived refuge
No longer issue passes for visitation
Throwaway minds lost in sanitation
Searching for cause
Applauses not deem-able
Researchable plans tampered
Justice is out of service
The former believer in purpose
Has no future
Reachers without push
Preachers no longer talk
God's will
They only speak of dollar bills
Strong minds on a steady decline

No truth in a land of lies
Flight bears no wings
Care has lost all its meaning
Feeding minds with lies
Newsflash
The news is a riot
Never knew TV was a pilot
Dreams of spaceships and skyrockets
Eyes caught in lint pockets
Blurred vision
Sight of new comets
No superstar
The only comet was the one in the bathroom
When nightmares wasn't enough
Reality hits
The site of no luck

No Superstar 2

The memories
Compressed air
Many tears
Across the chair lies a former energy
Crossed lakes of clarity
Water on the floor
A bad synergy
Once a worthy embassy
Now a travesty in the making
Every moment in life used to be breathtaking
Now heartbreak begins and ends each day
No matter what I say
The right thing is the wrong thing
And the wrong thing is a sure thing
Where have you gone clarity
The purest water has become dirty tap water
Order has no assembly
Chaos burning from my chimney
Is there a remedy for a pain of a once known superstar
Into a world of a reject
Yelling who we are
When in fact
I suffer alone
So who am I
No superstar
The perfect failure

No Superstar 3 (Wrong Mirror)

I am no longer the same
Once was a shining star
The reflection shines brighter no more
A dark clarity
Wisdom is a memory
Smoke the undying ecstasy
Black clouds surrounded with doubt
Led to the fatal exodus
Used to be a superstar
With scenes of Eden in my Genesis
Heard the news my mom was dying
So I have been writing ever since
Formally there were five senses
Now there is only one
What have I become
An unknown being
The mirror to my soul has no meaning
Escape is pleading
Release me
Used to dream
Now I scream verbally
Hoping for help
Emergency
Yet no one hears my cries
As I look to the sky
A former believer in rise
Now all I see is fallen skies

Faded pictures and broken promises
With a message
I am going to be what I am destined to be
No superstar
For I am garbage

Reflections

Ways like rivers part
No distance shall keep us apart
Alone in the dark
Reflections of a start
Silent as a heavy placed rock
Dreams on the spot
Martin's speech in the heart
Beams of radiant light glisten upon tree bark
Noise screeches from the wheels on shopping carts
Jumps in the car
Destination
Picnics at a park
The mystery beneath the cloth
A state of togetherness sharing deeper thoughts
Reflections
The mind's escape from narrow passages
Messages of false Intel
Government cells planted inside human brain cells
No teller of who is right
Sight placed in hands of clouded judgment
Innocents victimized
You are a bigger part of the system then you truly realize
Open eyes
Look past disguise
As flight takes place on heavens kite
Reflections

Day is night
Night is day
The season for treason
News is a fuse of false hope
Dis be true
Wins are losses
Losses are wins
For the moment of victory is when the winds change
Blown away like the gust
Memories become lost
Reflections of a start
Never again shall we part

Rise '13 (Today)

Today I lift myself up from the chains that bound me
Today I rise
For there are no boundaries
Legendary statuses used to be a figment of my imagination
But now imagination is my determination
And determination is the foundation
in which I lay rocks on
Ever since my moms gone
The sparks gone
Never felt sadness for so long
But today I rise
As my heart tells me to hold on
Keep strong
Stay warm
Pray more
As the sun rays gazes into these eyes
The truth behind the scenes comes alive
Cinematic thoughts from a distance
A surprise entry
The sunrise enters a once forever darkness
Destruction of night
Beginning of rise
For today I rise
As thoughts come to life
Oceans become openings
Locked doors welcome me

More than seldom I fall
But today I rise
Hoping my dreams won't fail me
I rise
I rise
I rise
For I have arrived

Rise '13 (Tomorrow)

My dreams today will be tomorrow's outcome
From the barrels of the slum
I am no longer from
Bread exists in pieces no more
As I am whole
Only pain knows my beginning
And even though sadness is winning
Still I smile
knowing a better tomorrow is on the horizon
Out of exile
A King arises from the Nile
I am the future
Yes I am the becoming
I rise to the sky of beautiful blue
As a foundation set in living proof
A testament of testimony
I am glory
Like the Kings and Queens before me
I rise like Martin did with his dream
So scream if you feel me
Clarity will you marry me
As I seek the throne of the majesty
No longer weak in jealousy
For I am plenty with inventory
My sword
My shield

The power to wield the will given to me
Still I rise eternally
To the graces of sun for all eternity

Seclusion

Love is an illusion
Hidden in a secluded space
A place called the heart
Why have we grown so far apart
Steps away from the light into darkness loom
Swept in its broom of deceit
Love played me like a vicious cheat
Blinded by its webs
Accompanied by fine legs
Had me spinning in circles
Jumping hurdles
Just to taste the inside of its girdle
Caught in the middle
With little information
Falsified documents
With condoms being served up as condiments

To complement the lies
Time flies as hearts die
Why reply
When on the inside I cry
Sigh
Relief
In the belief
I actually believed that love existed
And like a fool I kissed it
Took upon its nourishment
Hoping my spirit would flourish
Not be demolished
Friends since high school
Maybe if I would have studied in college
I would have understood her degree
With pain deeper than the sea
Love was not destined to be

She

She is the one that radiates light from the sun
Out from the shade
Risen out of graves
Having vital statistics
She is the key to my rebirth
Organized like research
Perched firmly on lofts
With a warmth as cool as the blissful spring
And a voice harmonious as the sing
She is the music that touches my life
Paintbrush
The drawings of a perfect being
Created from summer moments
A light made with heavens touch
Topped in sprinkle cones
In a world called her own
She is beauty magnetized by infinity
Her speech is a remedy for the listening ear
The air she breathes
Sets the tone for the coolest breeze
Her thoughts keep minds at ease
For when she releases
Captured is the most beautiful climax
At the climate of the highest temperature
On the horizon of being my new rise
She is one and only

Sleeping Tears

Your eyes are sleeping
My awakening is near
For in death
Dexterity will be made clear
The howls in the night
Bowels on the move
No more can I stomach this pain
As rain will pour its last shower
Over a lonely tower
Devour my soul
Empower the flame
Reunite what was lost once again
Bring joy
Show happiness
Just want know what it feels to be glad
Instead of being stuck in this bag
Trying to get ahead
In search for peace
Divisions of sleep
A remainder in tears
Forever in fear
Former cheers now turned jeers
Love ones don't fret
My awakening is near
For in death dexterity will be made clear
Your eyes are sleeping
Souls are weeping
Joy is losing
Pain is winning

Rain is coming
The end is only the beginning

Stage

Dream the dreams of dreamers
Light and sweet
No creamers
My glimmer shines brighter than hope
For I have seen the light
Been through struggles more than twice
Read the words of the wise
Witness plights and darker nights
Now I fly with greater sight
Elevation to the right
Revelation to the left
Salvation on the shelf
Foundation by the mills
Water in the wells
Kiss the girls
Never tell
Dust settles
The storm never will
Rain shall come
So the sleet can cry
Sheets will melt
For years heartbreak I felt
Take comfort in comforters
Knowing sleep is a loving resident
In my dreams
I dreamt

For a moment I was president
In another instance
I was an angel that was heaven sent
As I open my eyes
The ability to bend time and align stars
So far
Yet no distance will stop persistence
Evolving over dreams
No resistance
I awake to greatness
In the form of sun
To become leader for my future son

The Allure

The allure of Laura
Urkel dreams
Beams of clarity sent from beauty's stream
Truths of love and what it means
Unconditional showing
As the green that paints the grass
Thoughts in cabs
Destination surpassed
A mind contrasts
The bearer of luminous masks
To love
The formidable task
You ask
Simplicity is genuine misery
Pain the bearer of agape
Knowledge plucked from the juices of grapes
A warm touch
Hearts tucked deeply in crates
Visions of great lakes
Smoking mirrors
The holograms of repeated mistakes
Outbreaks of heartbreak
Her love was rich like the tasting of cheesecake
Misleading directions
Which way
Unverifiable circumstance

Misconception
The Jezebel affection
Ushering in
A throwback classic
My confession
I miss her

The Feeling

You know its close
When you could feel in your heart
Not knowing where to start
Everything whole is divided into parts
One word becomes many
A painting becomes an art
Distances from afar come closer
Like a star in the making
Every moment in life is breathtaking
Comparable to the greatest love
Worth waiting
A little patience will equal less stressing
Meaningful lessons will culminate into greater blessings
Beyond anything imaginable
Paradise like conditions
Happiness is the key
So are you up for the mission
The start of a brand new life
Addition
Your life pages becomes chapters
Edition
Former dreams are now realities
Defined by gravity
You are the center
Now enter

The Path

I can no longer cry no more
Tears have dried ashore
One thing is for sure
For many years I have been unsure
No more can I endure the pain
If cancer had a cure
My mother would carry on
With a heart as pure as gold
The feeling that I am alone remains
Love has left me in disdain
To regain my soul
In a room full of darkness
Where light never dimmers
My heart is screaming out FEMA
Part of me is gone
For so long feeling mourn
Many loved ones have died
Each attempt to rise
Has elevated these painful skies
So why feel anything
When I am still recovering
Recovering from the discovery
that I will never be the same again
The path of my optimistic
Has no tropic
The thesis of my life is a broken path
split into pieces
The rest is secret
Alone with a hurt

Perched on the skirt of a mountain
I have fallen
This is a recording
I am out

The Rose

The rose
Kisses from your thoughts exposed
The sweet mist from your body reveals the code
Unlocked passion bestowed
Who is the wearer of this dress
Treasurer thoughts
The mind is at sea
Pirates at the entrance waiting to seize the moment
Ripping of flesh
Bound in chain shackles
The rose still peaks my interest
From the greatest distances
Persistence allures my optimism
A new man transformed
The rose emanates the prime
Time has patience
Except for the rose
My patience grows thin
In want of her skin
To the very ends of the earth
I will search
Perched on mountain tops
Dreams of destiny
Dancing with a star
Epiphany
This rose and I are meant be

Forever
As love is proposed
Eyes will know
The day I fell in love with a rose

Used To

Used to be a winner
Now the air is thinner
All alone trapped in a cage
Mind blinded by rage
Life is a stage with performers
Everything begins and ends where it started
Used to have a part
Not used to this darkness
Too far away from the brightness
Hope is forever gone
All along thoughts were twisted
Hanging with the wicked
Never depicted scrutiny
Always wanted what was true to be
Eyes never woken
Not able to see
One who was quick to believe
So easily deceived
A soul that was lost
Needed to retrieve
But didn't understand the meaning of growth
Still a seed
In a field full of weeds
Always done what was a considered a good deed
Yet never reap the benefits
Instead faced with deficit

Dealing with life and its conflicts
A survivor of the projects
I am the subject of your negativity
When all I ever wanted was prosperity
I used to think of life as peaceful
Until my receipt read the words deceit
So it is
life has only one purpose
For you to crack like the concrete
Used to have dreams of starting a revolution
Incomplete is the mission
Defeat is your revelation
You are your own threat
Bomb
Detonation
Systems down
Malfunction
Used to function on our own wills
Then came death to which we all kneel

Victory

Eyes of enchantment
Flesh decomposed
Silent roses
The coming of winter
Pain deeper than physical
Spiritual spirits needed
Advice never heeded
A soul defeated
Searching for truth
Answers undefined
Dictionaries blind to the sublime
The end is only a beginner's line
Finding high in a state of why
Bending time
Moving twice
Backwards is life
Noted wise
Dwelling skies
Swelling eyes
A smell of rise
Sun is out
The pain is gone
Light has formed
Night is done
Knights will come to lead the run
Victory will be fed as one

Widow's Peak

Alive is what I feel
Peel the cap
Master can I have some of your sap
Daily is our nap
Steady dreaming as your back touches the pillow

The widow looks out from her window, and sees her husband's reflection through a blindfold. Holds his hand, and tells him my life without you is nothing more than a dying flame. Never could I love the same. In my brain I try but the pain never lies. As forever these tears will inherit these eyes. Forgive me for keeping our love a disguise. As the widow looks up to the sky, she wonders why? Why did I show resistance when you showed kindness? Is this meaning beyond my understanding? Help me God to see the error of my ways! As I pray for better days, I will only know faith for I have sinned. Where do I begin? Is this the story of my life? A wife who had love, yet was unable to grasp its meaning. I had defied life! For I have gone against the sacred provision known as marriage. To love a man who loved me to death. Was I the widow the cause of his death? There are many nights I cry as I weep in sadness. The memories I hold dear to my heart. Oh husband you have departed! You were my rock and my protection. The stable connection that kept me grounded. On the day you died, I found the meaning of true love.

So it goes
Highs and Lows
No matter the temperature
You gave me heat
Thus making my life complete

Love,

The Widow